David Holman

SELF RELIANT IS GIANT

"The Art of Self-Reliance: Navigating the 21st Century with Empowerment and Independence"

Table of Contents:

Chapter 1: Introduction

The 21st century has brought about countless changes and challenges, with one of the most signifcant being the need for self-reliance. In a rapidly evolving world, it has become increasingly important to take control of our lives and be self-suffcient. Whether it be in terms of fnances, health, career, or community, the ability to rely on oneself has become a crucial aspect of survival and success. This is why the topic of self-reliance is of such great signifcance in today's world.

Self-reliance is defned as the ability to rely on oneself to meet one's own needs and make decisions without relying on external help. It encompasses many different aspects of life, including fnancial stability, physical and emotional well-being, career development, community involvement, and more. When people are self-reliant, they are able to take control of their lives and make their own choices, which leads to a greater sense of independence and empowerment.

In this book, we will explore the different components of self-reliance and the ways in which they can be developed and strengthened. We will also look at the challenges that individuals face when trying to achieve self-reliance, and offer practical advice and strategies for overcoming these obstacles. By the end of this book, readers will have a better understanding of what self-reliance means, why it is so important, and how they can develop it in their own lives.

The topic of self-reliance is especially relevant in today's world because of the growing number of uncertainties and challenges that individuals face. With the global economy constantly in flux, job security has become a major concern for many people. The rise of automation and the gig economy has also made it more diffcult for individuals to achieve fnancial stability. In addition, there are also many physical and emotional challenges that individuals face, such as stress, anxiety, and chronic illness.

In light of these challenges, it has become increasingly important for people to be self-reliant. By relying on oneself, individuals can take control of their lives and make their own choices, which leads to a greater sense of independence and empowerment. They are also better equipped to navigate the uncertainties and challenges of life, and are more likely to achieve success and happiness.

In conclusion, self-reliance is a crucial aspect of survival and success in the 21st century. It encompasses many different components of life, including fnancial stability, physical and emotional well-being, career development, community involvement, and more. By exploring the different aspects of self-reliance and offering practical advice and strategies for developing it, this book aims to empower readers to take control of their lives and achieve greater independence and success.

- The benefts of self-reliance: Along with the sense of independence and empowerment that comes with self-reliance, there are also many practical benefts. For example, being self-reliant can lead to greater fnancial stability, better health and well-being, a fulflling career, and strong community connections.

- The role of technology: In today's world, technology has become a powerful tool for self-reliance. From online learning platforms to fnancial management apps, technology has made it easier for individuals to achieve self-reliance and independence. However, it is important to note that technology should be used as a tool and not a crutch.

- The importance of personal responsibility: To truly be self-reliant, individuals must take personal responsibility for their lives. This means making informed choices, taking action to achieve their goals, and being accountable for their actions and decisions. Personal responsibility is a key component of self-reliance and is essential for success.

- The role of self-awareness: To achieve self-reliance, individuals must have a clear understanding of their strengths and weaknesses, their values, and their goals. This requires self-awareness and introspection. By being self-aware, individuals are better equipped to make informed choices and take action to achieve their goals.

- The signifcance of community: While self-reliance requires individuals to rely on themselves, it is also important to have a strong support system and community connections. A supportive community can provide individuals with a sense of belonging, a network of resources, and a source of encouragement and motivation.

Chapter 2: Financial Self-Reliance

Financial self-reliance is a critical component of overall self-reliance. When individuals are fnancially self-reliant, they are able to take control of their fnances, meet their own needs, and make informed fnancial decisions. This leads to greater fnancial stability and independence, and reduces the need for external help or support.

The frst step towards fnancial self-reliance is to develop a solid understanding of personal fnances. This includes knowing how much money is coming in, how much is going out, and what debts and liabilities exist. Individuals should also have a clear understanding of their fnancial goals, such as saving for retirement, paying off debt, or building an emergency fund.

Once individuals have a clear understanding of their personal fnances, they can begin to take steps to improve their fnancial situation. This may involve reducing spending, increasing income, or seeking out fnancial advice and resources. In addition, it is important to develop good fnancial habits, such as saving regularly, avoiding debt, and investing in long-term fnancial products.

Technology has also made it easier for individuals to achieve fnancial self-reliance. There are now many fnancial management tools and apps that can help individuals track their spending, set fnancial goals, and make informed fnancial decisions. In addition, there are also many online learning resources, such as courses and blogs, that can help individuals improve their fnancial literacy and gain a deeper understanding of personal fnance.

Another important aspect of fnancial self-reliance is being able to manage risk. This means having a plan in place to protect against fnancial losses and setbacks, such as job loss, illness, or natural disasters. This may involve having an emergency fund, insurance, and other risk management strategies.

In conclusion, fnancial self-reliance is an essential component of overall self-reliance. By taking control of their fnances, individuals can achieve greater fnancial stability and independence, and reduce the need for external help or support. To achieve fnancial self-reliance, individuals must have a solid understanding of personal fnances, take steps to improve their fnancial situation, and develop good fnancial habits. In addition, technology and resources are available to help individuals achieve their fnancial goals, and managing risk is an important part of fnancial self-reliance.

- The impact of debt on fnancial self-reliance: Debt can have a signifcant impact on fnancial self-reliance. High levels of debt can limit an individual's ability to save, invest, and make informed fnancial decisions. It is important for individuals to understand the impact of debt on their fnances and to take steps to reduce or eliminate it.
- The importance of saving and investing: Saving and investing are key components of fnancial self-reliance. By saving regularly and investing in long-term fnancial products, individuals can build wealth, prepare for retirement, and achieve fnancial stability. It is important for individuals to understand the different types of savings and investment products available and to choose the products that are best suited to their needs and goals.
- The role of insurance: Insurance can play an important role in fnancial self-reliance by protecting against fnancial losses and setbacks. From health insurance to life insurance, there are many types of insurance that can help individuals achieve fnancial stability and independence. It is important for individuals to understand the different types of insurance available and to choose the products that are best suited to their needs and goals.
- The importance of a fnancial plan: Having a clear fnancial plan is an essential component of fnancial self-reliance. A fnancial plan can help individuals set fnancial goals, track their progress, and make informed fnancial decisions. A fnancial plan can also help individuals manage risk, protect against fnancial losses and setbacks, and achieve fnancial stability and independence.

Chapter 3: Health and Nutrition Self-Reliance

Maintaining good health and nutrition is a critical component of overall self-reliance. When individuals are healthy, they are better able to meet their own needs, pursue their goals, and live fulflling lives. In addition, good health and nutrition can improve overall well-being, reduce the risk of illness and disease, and increase lifespan.

The frst step towards health and nutrition self-reliance is to understand the body's nutritional needs. This includes knowing the types of nutrients the body requires, such as carbohydrates, proteins, fats, vitamins, and minerals, and the amounts of each that are needed for optimal health. In addition, individuals should understand the importance of a balanced diet, and the role that different food groups play in maintaining good health.

Another important aspect of health and nutrition self-reliance is knowing where to fnd the nutrients the body needs. This may involve eating a variety of foods, including fruits, vegetables, whole grains, lean proteins, and healthy fats. In addition, individuals should be familiar with food labeling, and know how to read and interpret nutrition information, such as calorie counts, serving sizes, and ingredient lists.

There are many resources available to help individuals achieve health and nutrition self-reliance. This may include online resources, such as nutrition websites and blogs, cookbooks, and nutrition apps. In addition, individuals can also seek out the advice and guidance of nutrition professionals, such as dietitians and nutritionists.

Technology has also played an important role in improving health and nutrition self-reliance. There are now many devices and tools, such as smart scales, ftness trackers, and nutrition monitoring apps, that can help individuals monitor their health and nutrition and make informed decisions about their diets

health and nutrition self-reliance is an essential component of overall self-reliance. By understanding the body's nutritional needs and knowing where to fnd the nutrients it needs, individuals can maintain good health, reduce the risk of illness and disease, and achieve greater overall well-being. In addition, technology and resources are available to help individuals achieve their health and nutrition goals and improve their overall quality of life.

health and nutrition self-reliance is an essential component of overall self-reliance. By understanding the body's nutritional needs and knowing where to fnd the nutrients it needs, individuals can maintain good health, reduce the risk of illness and disease, and achieve greater overall well-being. In addition, technology and resources are available to help individuals achieve their health and nutrition goals and improve their overall quality of life.

Vitamins and Supplements:

Vitamins and supplements are often used by individuals looking to achieve better health and nutrition. While they can be an effective way to supplement the diet, it is important to understand the role that they play, and to use them responsibly.

There are many different types of vitamins and supplements available, including multivitamins, individual vitamin and mineral supplements, and specialty supplements, such as probiotics, omega-3 fatty acids, and antioxidants. It is important to understand the specifc benefts of each type of supplement, and to choose the products that are best suited to your needs and goals.

In addition, it is important to understand that vitamins and supplements should not be used as a replacement for a balanced diet. A well-balanced diet should provide all of the nutrients that the body needs, and supplements should only be used to supplement the diet, not replace it.

It is also important to understand the potential risks of using vitamins and supplements. Some supplements can interact with prescription medications, and others may have harmful side effects. It is important to speak with your doctor before beginning any new supplement regimen, to ensure that it is safe and appropriate for your needs.

Exercise:

Physical activity is an essential component of good health and nutrition. Regular physical activity can help individuals maintain a healthy weight, improve cardiovascular health, and reduce the risk of chronic disease. It is important for individuals to understand the benefts of physical activity, and to incorporate it into their daily routines as a means of improving overall health and nutrition.

The value of exercise cannot be overstated. Not only does it help individuals maintain good physical health, but it also has numerous mental and emotional benefts. Regular physical activity has been shown to reduce stress, improve mood, and boost self-esteem. It is also an effective way to increase energy levels, improve sleep, and enhance overall quality of life.

Incorporating physical activity into your daily routine can be as simple as taking a walk, engaging in a hobby, or taking up a sport. The key is to fnd an activity that you enjoy, and to make it a part of your daily routine. Whether it's joining a local gym, taking up yoga, or just taking a daily walk, there are countless ways to incorporate physical activity into your life.

Different Types of Physical Activity:

Physical activity is an important part of good health and nutrition, and it is important to understand the benefts of different types of physical activity. There are many different types of physical activity, each of which can offer specifc benefts, and it is important to choose the activities that are best suited to your needs and goals.

Strength training is a type of physical activity that is designed to increase muscle mass and strength. This type of activity can help individuals build a stronger, more toned physique, and can improve overall physical health. Strength training can also improve bone density, and reduce the risk of osteoporosis and other chronic diseases.

Cardiovascular exercise, or cardio, is a type of physical activity that is designed to increase heart rate and improve cardiovascular health. This type of activity can help individuals burn calories, maintain a healthy weight, and improve their overall physical ftness. Examples of cardiovascular exercise include running, cycling, swimming, and jumping rope.

Flexibility exercises, such as yoga and stretching, are designed to increase flexibility, reduce muscle stiffness, and improve overall range of motion. This type of physical activity can help individuals reduce the risk of injury, and improve physical function and quality of life.

It is important to incorporate a variety of physical activities into your routine in order to achieve a balanced and well-rounded ftness regimen. For example, you might engage in strength training two or three times per week, and also participate in cardio and flexibility activities on a regular basis. By doing so, individuals can achieve their health and ftness goals, and improve their overall quality of life.

physical activity is an important part of good health and nutrition, and it is important to understand the benefts of different types of physical activity. Whether you choose strength training, cardio, or flexibility exercises, it is important to fnd activities that you enjoy, and to make them a part of your daily routine. By doing so, individuals can achieve their health and ftness goals, and improve their overall quality of life

Chapter 4: Financial Self-Reliance in the 21st Century

Financial self-reliance is an important aspect of being self-reliant in the 21st century. In today's world, it is more important than ever to have control over your fnancial situation, and to understand the ways in which you can achieve fnancial independence. This chapter will explore some of the key principles of fnancial self-reliance, and provide practical advice for achieving fnancial independence.

The frst step in achieving fnancial self-reliance is to understand your current fnancial situation. This means taking a close look at your income, expenses, and debts, and creating a realistic budget that accounts for your lifestyle and goals. It is important to be honest with yourself about your spending habits, and to make a conscious effort to reduce your expenses where possible.

Once you have a clear understanding of your current fnancial situation, it is time to focus on your goals. What do you want to achieve fnancially? Do you want to pay off debt, save for a home or retirement, or invest in stocks and bonds? By setting clear, specifc fnancial goals, you can create a roadmap for achieving fnancial independence.

Another key principle of fnancial self-reliance is to be proactive in your approach to saving and investing. This means taking advantage of opportunities to save money, such as by utilizing coupons and shopping for sales. It also means investing your money in a diversifed portfolio of stocks, bonds, and other assets, in order to maximize your returns over time.

In addition to saving and investing, it is also important to have a solid understanding of credit and debt. This means knowing your credit score, and taking steps to improve it where necessary. It also means avoiding high-interest debt, such as credit card debt, and focusing on paying down debt as quickly as possible.

Finally, it is important to be informed and engaged in your fnancial situation. This means staying up-to-date with news and developments in the fnancial world, and taking an active interest in your investments and fnancial portfolio. By staying informed and engaged, you can make informed decisions about your fnances, and take control of your fnancial future.

In conclusion, fnancial self-reliance is an important aspect of being self-reliant in the 21st century. By understanding your current fnancial situation, setting clear goals, being proactive in your approach to saving and investing, having a solid understanding of credit and debt, and staying informed and engaged, individuals can achieve fnancial independence and control over their fnancial future.

- Building an emergency fund: Having a savings account set aside specifcally for unexpected expenses is an important part of fnancial self-reliance. This fund can be used to pay for unexpected expenses, such as medical bills or car repairs, without having to rely on credit cards or loans.
- Understanding taxes: Tax laws can be complex and confusing, but it is important to have a basic understanding of how taxes work and how to minimize your tax burden. This includes taking advantage of tax deductions and credits, and knowing your tax obligations as a self-employed individual or small business owner.
- Retirement planning: Retirement planning is an important part of fnancial self-reliance, as it allows individuals to prepare for their fnancial future and ensure that they have enough money to support themselves in their later years. This includes understanding different types of retirement accounts, such as IRAs and 401(k)s, and developing a retirement savings plan that fts your individual needs and goals.
- Estate planning: Estate planning is the process of preparing for the distribution of your assets after your death. This includes developing a will, establishing trusts, and making plans for the distribution of your assets. Estate planning is an important part of fnancial self-reliance, as it helps to ensure that your assets are distributed according to your wishes and that your loved ones are taken care of after your death.
- Investing: Investing is an important part of fnancial self-reliance, as it allows individuals to grow their wealth and achieve their long-term fnancial goals. This includes understanding different types of investments, such as stocks, bonds, and mutual funds, and developing a diversifed investment portfolio that fts your individual needs and risk tolerance.
- Understanding debt: Debt can be a necessary part of fnancial self-reliance, but it is important to understand how to use debt wisely and avoid becoming overwhelmed by debt. This includes understanding different types of debt, such as credit card debt and student loans, and developing a debt repayment plan that helps you pay off debt as quickly as possible.

- Budgeting: Budgeting is an essential part of fnancial self-reliance, as it helps individuals track their spending and make informed decisions about their fnances. This includes creating a budget, tracking your expenses, and regularly reviewing your budget to ensure that you are staying on track and making progress towards your fnancial goals.
- Building wealth: Building wealth is the process of accumulating assets and increasing your net worth over time. This includes understanding the concept of compounding and how to use it to your advantage, developing a savings plan, and making informed decisions about your fnances that support your long-term fnancial goals.

By covering these topics and others, individuals can gain a comprehensive understanding of fnancial self-reliance and develop the skills and knowledge they need to achieve their fnancial goals and build a secure fnancial future.

Chapter 5, titled "Building Strong Relationships: The Key to Emotional Self-Reliance":

Building strong relationships with others is a crucial aspect of emotional self-reliance. Having a supportive network of friends, family, and loved ones can provide individuals with a sense of belonging, help them to cope with challenges, and provide them with the emotional support they need to thrive.

One of the most important aspects of building strong relationships is effective communication. This includes listening actively, expressing oneself clearly, and being open and honest with others. Effective communication can help to build trust and understanding in relationships, and can help individuals to resolve conflicts and work through challenges together.

Another important aspect of building strong relationships is empathy. Empathy involves understanding and sharing the feelings of others, and it is a key component of healthy relationships. By showing empathy towards others, individuals can build stronger connections and foster deeper levels of understanding and trust.

In addition to communication and empathy, building strong relationships also requires time and effort. This includes setting aside time for relationships, being present and engaged when with others, and being willing to make sacrifces for the sake of the relationship. Building strong relationships requires patience and persistence, but the rewards are well worth the effort.

Lastly, it is important to recognize the importance of self-care in building strong relationships. This includes taking care of one's own physical, emotional, and mental well-being, and seeking support when needed. By prioritizing self-care, individuals can maintain their own emotional stability and resilience, and be better equipped to support and care for others in their relationships.

Cultivating a growth mindset is a key component of personal growth and development, and it is essential for individuals who seek to be self-reliant. A growth mindset is characterized by a belief in one's ability to grow and develop, and a willingness to embrace challenges as opportunities for growth and learning.

One of the most important aspects of cultivating a growth mindset is a willingness to learn and try new things. This includes seeking out new experiences and taking on new challenges, even if they are outside of one's comfort zone. By pushing oneself to try new things, individuals can expand their skills and knowledge, and build their confdence and resilience.

Another important aspect of cultivating a growth mindset is embracing failure. Failure is an inevitable part of growth and learning, and it is important to view failures as opportunities for growth, rather than as setbacks. By embracing failure, individuals can develop a growth mindset and learn to bounce back from setbacks, building their resilience and determination.

It is also important to cultivate a positive attitude and a sense of purpose in life. This includes setting goals, developing a sense of direction and purpose, and focusing on one's strengths and abilities. By having a clear sense of purpose and direction, individuals can cultivate a growth mindset and stay motivated and focused on their personal growth and development.

Lastly, it is important to seek out support and resources to help with personal growth and development. This includes seeking out mentorship, coaching, and education opportunities, as well as seeking support from friends, family, and loved ones. By seeking out support and resources, individuals can cultivate a growth mindset and achieve their personal growth and development goals.

By focusing on learning, embracing failure, cultivating a positive attitude and sense of purpose, and seeking support, individuals can cultivate a growth mindset and achieve their personal growth and development goals, becoming more self-reliant in the process.

Chapter 6, titled "The Main Principles of Self-Reliance in the 21st Century":

In the previous chapters, we have explored various aspects of being self-reliant in the 21st century, including personal fnance, health and wellness, and personal growth and development. In this fnal chapter, we will summarize the main principles of self-reliance that have been discussed throughout the book.

1. Financial literacy and independence: One of the key principles of being self-reliant is to have a strong understanding of personal fnance, including budgeting, saving, investing, and managing debt. By developing fnancial literacy, individuals can take control of their fnancial future and achieve fnancial independence.

2. Health and wellness: Another important principle of self-reliance is to prioritize health and wellness. This includes maintaining a balanced diet, engaging in physical activity, and seeking regular medical care when necessary. By prioritizing health and wellness, individuals can improve their overall quality of life and reduce their dependence on others.

3. Personal growth and development: Cultivating a growth mindset is a key component of personal growth and development, and it is essential for individuals who seek to be self-reliant. By embracing learning and challenges, embracing failure, cultivating a positive attitude and sense of purpose, and seeking support, individuals can achieve their personal growth and development goals.

4. Resourcefulness and adaptability: In the rapidly changing world of the 21st century, being resourceful and adaptable is crucial for self-reliance. This includes being able to effectively manage resources, fnd new solutions to problems, and adapt to changing circumstances.

5. Independence and self-suffciency: Finally, self-reliance means being independent and self-suffcient. This includes being able to provide for oneself, taking control of one's life, and making decisions that align with one's values and goals.

6. Financial Literacy and Independence: Financial literacy and independence are critical components of being self-reliant in the 21st century. Financial literacy involves understanding basic fnancial concepts such as budgeting, saving, investing, and managing debt. By developing fnancial literacy, individuals can take control of their fnancial future, achieve fnancial independence, and reduce their dependence on others.

For example, by creating a budget and sticking to it, individuals can better understand their income and expenses, and prioritize their spending in line with their goals. Additionally, by saving and investing, individuals can build wealth over time and secure their fnancial future. Furthermore, by managing debt effectively, individuals can reduce fnancial stress and avoid falling into debt traps.

1. Health and Wellness: Health and wellness are essential for overall well-being and play a critical role in being self-reliant. This involves maintaining a balanced diet, engaging in physical activity, and seeking regular medical care when necessary. By prioritizing health and wellness, individuals can improve their overall quality of life, increase their energy and resilience, and reduce their dependence on others.

For example, a balanced diet that includes a variety of fruits, vegetables, whole grains, lean proteins, and healthy fats provides the body with the nutrients it needs to function properly. Regular physical activity, such as running, yoga, or weightlifting, can help maintain physical health and reduce the risk of chronic diseases. Additionally, regular medical check-ups can help individuals stay informed about their health status and address any potential health concerns early on.

1. Personal Growth and Development: Personal growth and development are key components of being self-reliant, and involve cultivating a growth mindset, embracing learning and challenges, cultivating a positive attitude and sense of purpose, and seeking support. By embracing these principles, individuals can achieve their personal growth and development goals and increase their independence and self-suffciency.

For example, by embracing challenges, individuals can increase their resilience, overcome obstacles, and develop new skills and knowledge. Cultivating a positive attitude and sense of purpose can help individuals maintain motivation, focus on their goals, and avoid distractions. Seeking support from friends, family, or a support group can provide individuals with encouragement, guidance, and accountability as they work towards their goals.

1. Resourcefulness and Adaptability: Resourcefulness and adaptability are critical components of self-reliance in the 21st century, as the world is rapidly changing and individuals must be able to effectively manage resources and fnd new solutions to problems. By being resourceful and adaptable, individuals can increase their independence and self-suffciency, and reduce their dependence on others.

For example, being resourceful may involve fnding creative solutions to problems, such as using recycled materials to create new products, or fnding alternative sources of energy to reduce dependence on fossil fuels. Adaptability may involve embracing new technologies, learning new skills, or adapting to new work environments, such as remote work. By being resourceful and adaptable, individuals can stay ahead of the curve and maintain their independence and self-suffciency.

1. Independence and Self-Suffciency: Independence and self-suffciency are the ultimate goals of self-reliance, and involve being able to provide for oneself, taking control of one's life, and making decisions that align with one's values and goals. By embracing independence and self-suffciency, individuals can achieve greater autonomy, personal fulfllment, and overall well-being.

For example, by being independent, individuals can make decisions that align with their values and goals, such as pursuing a career that aligns with their

Self-reliance is a journey, not a destination. As you continue to cultivate this quality in yourself, it's essential to stay focused on the main principles that guide this lifestyle. In this chapter, we will go over fve of the most important principles of self-reliance.

1. Responsibility: Self-reliant individuals take responsibility for their lives and the choices they make. They understand that their decisions and actions have consequences, both positive and negative, and they're willing to accept these consequences without blaming others. They take responsibility for their health, their fnances, and their relationships, and they are proactive in seeking solutions to the problems that arise.

2. Resilience: Self-reliant individuals are resilient, meaning they have the ability to bounce back from setbacks and challenges. They have a strong sense of self-worth and a positive outlook on life that helps them to weather the storms of life and come out even stronger on the other side. They are proactive in seeking out support and resources when they need it, but they don't rely on others to solve their problems for them.

3. Resourcefulness: Self-reliant individuals are resourceful, meaning they are able to fnd creative solutions to the challenges they face. They don't wait for someone else to solve their problems; they take the initiative to fnd solutions themselves. They are skilled at repurposing and upcycling, and they are able to fnd ways to stretch their resources to meet their needs.

4. Self-suffciency: Self-reliant individuals strive for self-suffciency, meaning they have the ability to take care of their basic needs without relying on others. They grow their own food, generate their own power, and are skilled at repairing and maintaining their possessions. They understand the importance of developing skills that are useful in everyday life, such as basic carpentry, sewing, and cooking.

5. Sustainability: Self-reliant individuals understand the importance of sustainability, meaning they take a long-term view of their impact on the environment and the world around them. They strive to live in a way that conserves resources, reduces waste, and protects the natural environment. They understand that the choices they make today will have an impact on the world their children and grandchildren will inherit, and they work to leave a positive legacy for future generations.

In conclusion, self-reliance is about taking control of your life and taking responsibility for your actions and choices. By focusing on the main principles of responsibility, resilience, resourcefulness, self-suffciency, and sustainability, you can create a life that is rich, fulflling, and truly self-reliant.

Conclusion and Summary

Self-reliance is a valuable quality in the 21st century. By taking control of your life and taking responsibility for your actions and choices, you can create a life that is rich, fulflling, and truly self-reliant. In this book, we explored various aspects of self-reliance, including personal fnance, health and nutrition, exercise, self-suffciency, and the main principles that guide this lifestyle.

The principles of self-reliance, including responsibility, resilience, resourcefulness, self-suffciency, and sustainability, serve as a roadmap for a fulflling life. By focusing on these principles, you can create a life that is rich in meaning and purpose. Whether you are looking to live a more sustainable life, to be more self-suffcient, or to simply have more control over your life, the principles of self-reliance provide a path to achieve these goals.

In this book, we discussed the importance of personal fnance and the steps you can take to become more fnancially self-reliant. We explored the benefts of a healthy diet and the importance of exercise for both physical and mental well-being. We also discussed the importance of developing self-suffciency skills, such as gardening, carpentry, and sewing, and the role of sustainability in creating a better future for ourselves and future generations.

In conclusion, self-reliance is a journey, not a destination. By focusing on the main principles of self-reliance, you can create a life that is rich, fulflling, and truly self-reliant. The principles of responsibility, resilience, resourcefulness, self-suffciency, and sustainability provide a roadmap for a meaningful and purposeful life. By embracing these principles and putting them into practice, you can create a life that is truly self-reliant and truly your own.

As we have seen throughout this book, self-reliance is a multi-faceted concept that touches every aspect of our lives. From our fnancial independence to our physical and mental well-being, self-reliance requires us to take control of our lives and to make conscious decisions about how we want to live. The principles of self-reliance, including responsibility, resilience, resourcefulness, self-suffciency, and sustainability, serve as a guide for creating a life that is fulflling and meaningful.

In terms of practical tips for developing self-reliance, it is important to remember that progress is made through small steps and consistent effort. Whether you are working to improve your fnancial situation, your health, or your self-suffciency skills, it is essential to be patient and persistent. It is also important to seek out resources and support when needed, whether that means seeking the advice of a fnancial advisor, connecting with others who share your interests in self-suffciency, or seeking professional help with your health and wellness journey.

Another key aspect of self-reliance is the importance of developing a strong sense of purpose. By defning what is truly important to you and setting goals that align with your values, you can create a life that is meaningful and fulflling. Whether it is through volunteering, pursuing your passions, or building relationships with loved ones, fnding your purpose and staying true to your values will help you to maintain your self-reliance journey, even in the face of adversity.

In conclusion, self-reliance is not just about being independent, it is about creating a life that is truly your own. By embracing the principles of self-reliance, you can cultivate a life that is rich in meaning, purpose, and fulfllment. Whether you are just starting your journey, or you have been on the path for some time, there is always more to learn and more to experience as you continue to deepen your self-reliance practice. With determination, patience, and a commitment to growth, the rewards of self-reliance are truly endless.

www.ingramcontent.com/pod-product-compliance
Lightning Source LLC
Chambersburg PA
CBHW051727250726

48653CB00008B/3249